THANK YOU, Sarah

The Woman Who Saved Thanksgiving

Laurie Halse Anderson

Matt Faulkner

SCHOLASTIC INC.

New York Toronto London Auckland Sydney
Mexico City New Delhi Hong Kong Buenos Aires

ISBN 0-439-56978-8

12 11 10 9 8 7 6 5 4 3 2   3 4 5 6 7 8/0

Printed in the U.S.A.   40

First Scholastic printing, September 2003

Book design by Mark Siegel

The text for this book is set in Caslon Old Face.

Illustrator's Note:
I had a lot of fun drawing and painting Sarah Hale and her world. Sarah was a complex person—powerful yet refined, dynamic, humorous, and even, perhaps, eccentric. Just my kind of lady. I started working on the book after September 11, 2001. A difficult time for everyone. I found a great deal of comfort in the example of Sarah's life. Her tenacity and style in the face of great difficulties were very inspiring to me.

The illustrations are rendered in India ink, colored inks, watercolor and gouache
on 140 lb. Arches cold-pressed paper.

To Alyssa Eisner, who knows a good idea when she sees one
—L. H. A.

For my nieces and nephews—
Isabella, Sydney, Becky, Jordan, Clancy, Casey, Keith, and Fletcher
—M. F.

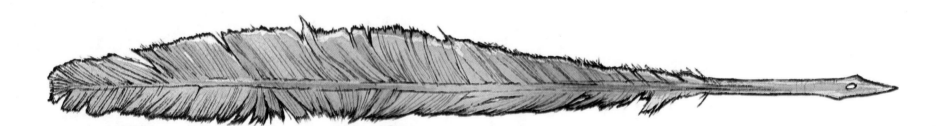

You think you know everything about Thanksgiving, don't you? . . . How the Native Americans saved the Pilgrims from starving. . . .

How the Pilgrims held a big feast to celebrate and say thank you: turkey, pumpkin pie, cranberries—the works.

Well, listen up. I have a news flash. . . .

Didn't know that, did you? It's true. Way, way back, when skirts were long and hats were tall, Thanksgiving was fading away. Sure, the folks up in New England celebrated it. They'd roast a turkey and invite the relatives when the harvest came in. But not in the South, not in the West, not even in the Middle Atlantic states. More and more, people ignored the holiday.

New England

The Mid-Atlantic

The West

The South

Thanksgiving was in trouble.
It needed . . .

A SUPERHERO!

No, not that kind.

Thanksgiving needed a *real* superhero, someone bold and brave and stubborn and smart.

Thanksgiving needed
Sarah Hale.

Now, I know what you're
thinking. She doesn't look
like a superhero. She looks
like a dainty little lady.

Never underestimate
dainty little ladies.

Sarah Hale was every inch a superhero. Not only did she fight for Thanksgiving, she fought for playgrounds for kids, schools for girls, and historical monuments for everyone.

GIRLS AND BOYS SCHOOL

She argued against spanking,
pie for breakfast, dull stories,
corsets and bloomers and bustles,

and very serious things like slavery.

As if that weren't enough, she raised five children; wrote poetry, children's books, novels, and biographies; was the first female magazine editor in America; published great American authors like Henry Wadsworth Longfellow and Edgar Allan Poe; and composed "Mary Had a Little Lamb."

How did she do all of these things?

She was bold, brave, stubborn, and smart. And Sarah Hale had a secret weapon . . .

a pen.

When Sarah saw something she didn't like, she picked up her pen and wrote about it. She wrote letters. She wrote articles. She wrote and wrote and wrote until she persuaded people to make the world a better place.

Nothing stopped Sarah.

Sarah Hale loved Thanksgiving. She wanted the whole country to celebrate it on the same day. When folks started to ignore Thanksgiving, well, that just curdled her gravy.

She picked up her pen.

Sarah wrote letters, thousands of letters, asking
politicians to make Thanksgiving a national holiday. She
wrote magazine articles asking her readers for help.

The women of America listened. They put down their babies, their hoes, their skillets, and their washing. They picked up their pens and wrote.

When the letters arrived, the politicians listened, too. One by one, the states officially made Thanksgiving a holiday. But that wasn't good enough. Sarah Hale wanted the whole country to celebrate together, like a family.

She went to the top.

Sarah wrote to the president
himself, Zachary Taylor.
He refused. Did that stop Sarah?
No! She waited for the next election
and wrote to the new president,
Millard Fillmore.
He said no, too.

Did that stop Sarah?
No! She was bold, brave,
stubborn, and smart.
Sarah wrote to the next
president, Franklin Pierce.
Wouldn't a national day of
thanksgiving be wonderful?

No, Pierce
grumped.

Sarah penned an elegant letter to President James Buchanan. She gave all the reasons why America would be better off if everyone gathered on the fourth Thursday in November to give thanks.

President Buchanan disagreed.

He had other things on his mind.

Sarah felt like the stuffing had been kicked out of her. Everything was going wrong.

America was at war, the North against the South. States that had promised to celebrate Thanksgiving changed their mind. The country was falling apart. It was a bleak and scary time.

Did that stop Sarah?

No way! Nothing stopped Sarah!
Superheroes work the hardest
when things get tough.
She picked up her mighty pen and
wrote another letter, this time to
President Abraham Lincoln.
America needed
Thanksgiving, now more
than ever. A holiday wouldn't
stop the war, but it could
help bring the country
together.
She signed the letter, folded it,
and slid it into an envelope.
She wrote Mr. Lincoln's name
and address on the envelope
and stuck on a stamp. She
mailed the letter.

She waited.

And she waited.

And then . . .

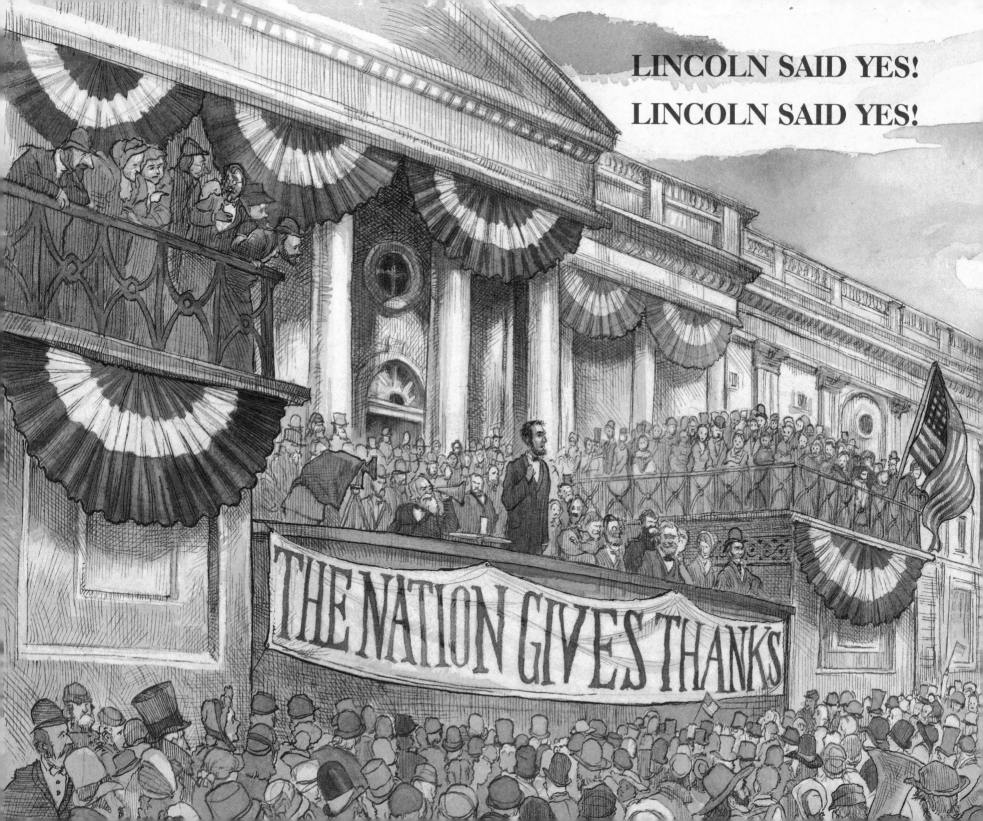

LINCOLN SAID YES!
LINCOLN SAID YES!

THE NATION GIVES THANKS

In 1863 President Lincoln made Thanksgiving a national holiday—a day for all Americans to give thanks, together. It took Sarah Hale thirty-eight years, thousands of letters, and countless bottles of ink, but she did it. Nothing stopped Sarah. That bold, brave, stubborn, and smart lady saved Thanksgiving . . . for all of us.

THANK YOU, SARAH!

TRADITION PRESERVED

The Thanksgiving we celebrate today is based on the harvest feast held by the Pilgrims in 1621. But the Pilgrims did not invent Thanksgiving. Celebrations of thanksgiving have been held all over the world for centuries.

GOOD STOCK

Historians believe that the first European Thanksgiving in North America took place on the coast of Florida in 1513. Spanish explorer Juan Ponce de León declared the day of thanks after successfully crossing the Atlantic. On May 23, 1541, another explorer from Spain, Francisco Vásquez de Coronado, held a Thanksgiving service in Texas. Several other days of Thanksgiving were celebrated in the South and Southwest in the 1500s, and along the Atlantic coast in the early 1600s.

By the mid-1600s, the colonists of New England were holding annual harvest festivals. These festivals were derived from the Pilgrims' Thanksgiving. The crops were in, the storehouses were full, and the community was ready for the winter. Each community decided for itself when Thanksgiving would be held. Everything depended on the weather and the timing of the harvest.

During the Revolutionary War, the Continental Congress declared seven days of thanksgiving. These were religious days of prayer, not family gatherings or feasts. In 1789, President George Washington issued a national proclamation that declared the last Thursday in November a "Day of Thanksgiving and prayer." When Sarah Hale lobbied for the revitalization of the holiday, she used the date chosen by Washington.

Every president after Lincoln continued the tradition of declaring the fourth Thursday in November to be Thanksgiving. Every president until Franklin Delano Roosevelt.

In 1939, America was suffering from the Great Depression. Millions of people were out of work. A group of business owners, the National Retail Dry Goods Association, asked President Roosevelt to lengthen the holiday shopping season by moving Thanksgiving up one week. Roosevelt agreed. In 1939 and 1940, Thanksgiving was held on the *third* Thursday in November.

People were outraged. The country split down the middle about what they called "Franksgiving." Twenty-three states went along with Roosevelt. Twenty-three states refused and celebrated instead on the traditional date. Two states, Colorado and Texas, celebrated on both Thursdays!

In the spring of 1941, Roosevelt announced that the experiment had failed. Despite a longer shopping season, holiday sales had not increased. Congress passed a joint resolution declaring once and for all that Thanksgiving would be celebrated on the fourth Thursday in November. Roosevelt signed the bill into law. Thanksgiving was finally safe.

EXTRA HELPINGS: FOOTBALL AND PARADES

Football was played on Thanksgiving Day for the first time in the 1870s. It quickly became a tradition, particularly for Ivy League teams. By the 1890s the Princeton-Yale game was attracting crowds of forty thousand spectators.

Within five years there were more than five thousand Thanksgiving Day football games being played by high school and college teams. Church services were moved earlier in the day to accommodate sports fans. In 1893 a newspaper editorial declared: "Thanksgiving Day is no longer a solemn festival to God for mercies given. . . . It is a holiday granted by the State and the Nation to see a game of football."

The first Macy's parade took place in 1924. It was organized by store employees and had floats, bands, and animals from the Central Park Zoo. The first helium balloons were carried in the parade in 1927. For many families, watching Thanksgiving Day parades is as much a part of celebrating the holiday as turkey and pumpkin pie.

Vintage America, 1863

- Mail is delivered free of charge for the first time in large cities.
- "When Johnny Comes Marching Home" is composed by Patrick S. Gilmore (a.k.a. Louis Lambert).
- The first breakfast cereal, called Granula, is invented by Dr. James Caleb Jackson.
- Roller skates, invented by James Plimpton, become very popular.
- Susan B. Anthony and Elizabeth Cady Stanton form the National Woman's Loyal League to collect signatures for the adoption of the Thirteenth Amendment to abolish slavery.

January 1—The Emancipation Proclamation technically frees all slaves. In reality, millions are still held in bondage.

January 26—The secretary of war allows African Americans to serve in the Union army. More than 200,000 take advantage of the offer.

February 24—The territory of Arizona is established.

March 3—The Draft Act is passed to draft men for the war.

July 1–3—The Battle of Gettysburg: More than fifty thousand men are killed or wounded.

July 13–16—The Draft Riots erupt in New York City.

July 30—Henry Ford is born.

October 3—Abraham Lincoln declares the fourth Thursday in November as national Thanksgiving.

October 27—The first tracks for the transcontinental railroad are laid in Sacramento, California.

November 19—Lincoln delivers the Gettysburg Address to dedicate the military cemetery at the battlefield.

November 26—Thanksgiving is celebrated.

December—Soldiers led by Kit Carson force Navajo leaders to surrender to U.S. troops. More than eight thousand Navajo are forced to walk 350 miles to a prison camp, where they are held for three years. Thousands die.

Bitter Fruit: The Civil War and Slavery

In 1861 a group of Southern states decided they no longer wanted to belong to the United States of America. They seceded (split off) and declared themselves independent. This was the beginning of the Civil War.

There were many reasons for the split. The Northern states (the Union) had developed an industrial economy, while the Southern states (the Confederacy) remained largely agricultural. Millions of Europeans immigrated to the North, seeking jobs in factories and mills. The South relied on the labor of slaves. As the economies of the two regions went in different directions, the culture and popular opinions of Northerners and Southerners split, too. It was illegal to own slaves in the North. In the South, however, 3.5 *million* African Americans were enslaved.

The simmering tensions boiled over when western territories asked to be recognized as states. The North wanted these territories to be Free States, where it would be illegal to own slaves. The South wanted more slave states. After years of arguing in Congress, the South declared its independence. The North said they couldn't go. The two sides fought for years. And in the end the country reunited.

On December 6, 1865, the Thirteenth Amendment to the Constitution was ratified. It said that "neither Slavery, nor involuntary servitude" was allowed in the United States. Slavery had ended.

HAIL TO THE CHEF! SARAH JOSEPHA BUELL HALE

Daughter of the Revolution

Sarah Josepha Buell Hale was born on October 24, 1788. Her father, Gordon Buell, was a disabled veteran of the Revolutionary War. Sarah grew up listening to her father's patriotic stories of the war. They made a deep impression on her.

The Buell family lived on a farm outside Newport, New Hampshire. Gordon's war wounds made farmwork difficult. When his sons left for college, he sold the farm and bought a small inn in town. Sarah helped out by teaching local children.

Teacher

One day a lamb followed one of Sarah's students to school. The lamb waited outside the schoolhouse for its owner all day. Sarah wrote a poem about the incident called "Mary Had a Little Lamb," which became one of the most famous nursery rhymes in America.

Sarah married a young lawyer named David Hale in 1813. David loved books as much as Sarah did. The two were very happy until David died of pneumonia when Sarah was pregnant with their fifth child. Sarah wore black mourning dresses for the rest of her life.

To feed her family, Sarah took a job making hats. At night, when her children were sleeping, she wrote poetry and worked on a novel. After five years she published her first novel, *Northwood*. A publisher read the book and offered Sarah a job at a new magazine, called the *Ladies' Magazine*. Sarah accepted.

Editor

The *Ladies' Magazine* was a hit. It was the most popular magazine for American women. For the first time American women could participate in mass culture. Sarah Hale understood this. She realized she was in a powerful and important position. She was an opinion maker.

The magazine was a blend of fashions, household advice, and educational articles. Alongside recipes for asparagus, readers found essays about ancient Rome. Pictures of the latest French fashions alternated with poetry and short stories. Sarah published some of the most famous authors of her day: Edgar Allan Poe, Harriet Beecher Stowe, Nathaniel Hawthorne, Henry Wadsworth Longfellow, Lydia M. Child, Frances Hodgson Burnett, Washington Irving, and Charles Dickens. And every issue had an editorial from Sarah advocating her causes, such as the quest for a national Thanksgiving.

One thing Sarah did not support was the growing women's movement. She disagreed strongly with women like Elizabeth Cady Stanton and Susan B. Anthony. Sarah Hale believed women should be educated, but she did not think men and women were equal. She thought there were men's activities and women's activities, and they rarely overlapped.

Most scholars believe Sarah Hale saw herself as upholding the traditional role of women in America. By encouraging women to read, educate their children, make a nice home, and support their husband, Sarah was doing what her own mother had done. In many ways her life mirrored that of Queen Victoria, whom she greatly admired. Victoria became the queen of the British Empire in 1837, the same year Sarah went to work at another magazine, *Godey's Lady's Book*. Both women were devoted to their family, both were widowed, and both were extremely influential. They saw themselves as traditional women, even though they lived untraditional lives.

Although she didn't call herself a women's rights advocate, Sarah Hale was very important to the women's rights movement. She pushed hard for the education of girls, for women's colleges, for female doctors and teachers, and for safe working conditions for all women. Sarah was against slavery, too, but she was not allowed to speak out about it in *Godey's*. Her publisher, Louis Godey, didn't want any politics in his magazine.

Last Days

By the time she was seventy-five, Sarah was working from her home. She continued to edit the magazine and write a steady stream of books and articles until her retirement in 1877, when she was eighty-nine years old. She wrote to her readers: "And now, having reached my ninetieth year, I must bid farewell to my countrywomen, with the hope that this work of half a century may be blessed. . . . New avenues for higher culture and for good works are opening before them, which fifty years ago were unknown. That they may improve these opportunities, and be faithful to their high vocation, is my heartfelt prayer."

Sarah kept writing letters and poetry until her death on April 30, 1879. She died in her ninetieth year, a daughter of the American Revolution who changed the country with her ideas.

Sarah Josepha Buell Hale lived in an era when most people treated women as second-class citizens. Women couldn't vote until 1920, forty-one years after Sarah died. Yet she was able to influence an entire nation through her writing.

Some people think that children have no power because they can't vote. Wrong. Children have a great deal of influence. They can write to newspaper editors and government representatives, petition community leaders, and lobby Congress.

Pick up your pen.
Change the world.

"*The pen is mightier than the sword.*"

—Edward Bulwer-Lytton

Selected Sources

Berlin, Ira, Marc Favreau, and Steven F. Miller, *Remembering Slavery: African-Americans Talk About Their Personal Experiences of Slavery and Emancipation.* New York: New Press, 1998.

Bird, Caroline. *Enterprising Women.* New York: Norton, 1976.

Feelings, Tom. *The Middle Passage: White Ships, Black Cargo.* New York: Dial Books, 1995.

Finley, Ruth E. *The Lady of Godey's: Sarah Josepha Hale.* Philadelphia: J. B. Lippincott, 1931.

Fryatt, Norma R. *Sarah Josepha Hale: The Life and Times of a Nineteenth-Century Career Woman.* New York: Hawthorn Books, 1975.

Godey's Lady's Book, various editions.

Hale, Sarah Josepha. *Manners; or, Happy Homes and Good Society All the Year Round.* Boston: J. E. Tilton, 1868.

——. *Northwood.* 2d. ed. New York: H. Long & Brother, 1852.

Holzer, Harold, compiler and editor, *Dear Mr. Lincoln: Letters to the President.* Reading, Mass.: Addison-Wesley, 1993.

Jacobson, Doranne, *The Civil War In Art,* New York: Smithmark Publishing, 1996.

Katcher, Philip, *American Civil War Artillery 1861-1865,* Oxford: Osprey Publishing, 2001.

Kunhardt, Philip, B., *Lincoln—An Illustrated Biography,* New York: Gramercy Publishing, 1999.

Lapsley, Arthur, editor, *Thanksgiving Proclamation: The Writings of Abraham Lincoln,* vol. 6. The Lamb Publishing Company, 1906.

Murdoch, David, *Eyewitness: North American Indian,* New York: Dorling Kindersley Publishing, 2000.

Pleck, Elizabeth H. *Celebrating the Family: Ethnicity, Consumer Culture, and Family Rituals.* Cambridge Mass.: Harvard University Press, 2000.

Plimoth-on-Web (www.plimoth.org). Official Web site of Plimoth Plantation, the living-history Museum of seventeenth-century Plymouth.

Pritzker, B. *Matthew Brady,* Hong Kong: Brompton Books, 1992.

Rogers, Sherbrooke. *Sarah Josepha Hale: A New England Pioneer, 1788–1879.* Grantham, N.H.: Tompson & Rutter, 1985.

Stanchack, John, E., *The Visual Dictionary of the Civil War,* New York: Dorling Kindersley Publishing, 2000.

Waters, Kate, *Tapenum's Day—A Wampanoag Indian Boy in Pilgrim Times,* New York: Scholastic Press, 1996.

Wheeler, Edmund. *The History of Newport, New Hampshire from 1766 to 1878.* Concord, N.H.: Republican Press Association,1879.

Acknowledgments

The author would like to say a big THANK YOU to the following:

Dr. Elizabeth H. Pleck, Department of History, University of Illinois at Urbana-Champaign, for offering some much needed advice.

The wonderful staff of the Richards Free Library of Newport, New Hampshire, Sarah Hale's hometown. I think Sarah would be very proud of your collection.

Dorset Colony House, Dorset, Vermont, for providing the author with peace and quiet.

Amy Berkower of Writers House, agent extraordinaire.

My family, as always—Greg, Meredith, and Stephanie—for your love and acceptance.

Dr. Lark Hall of the University of Pennsylvania.

The illustrator would like to thank Kevin Lewis and Alyssa Eisner, the book editors, and Mark Siegel, the book designer, for their enthusiasm, guidance, and support. It was a pleasure working with them. And thanks to Laurie Halse Anderson for the great research information about Sarah, which she supplied when I was working on the sketches.